Higher education as self-forma

Simon Marginson

IOE Press

Higher education as self-formation

Simon Marginson

Based on an Inaugural Professorial Lecture delivered at the UCL Institute of Education on 29 November 2017

UCL Institute of Education Press
Professorial Lecture Series

Institute of Education

First published in 2018 by the UCL Institute of Education Press,
20 Bedford Way, London WC1H 0AL

www.ucl-ioe-press.com

British Library Cataloguing-in-Publication Data:
A catalogue record for this publication is available from the British Library

ISBNs
978-1-78277-237-8 (Paperback)
978-1-78277-238-5 (PDF eBook)
978-1-78277-239-2 (ePub eBook)
978-1-78277-240-8 (Kindle eBook)

Typeset by Quadrant Infotech (India) Pvt Ltd
Printed by ImageData Ltd.

Biography

Simon Marginson joined the UCL Institute of Education (IOE) in 2013, prior to which he was based at the universities of Melbourne and Monash. He is one of the most cited researchers in the field of higher education studies.

Professor Marginson draws on and integrates a range of social science disciplines in his work, primarily political economy and political philosophy, historical sociology and social theory. His work focuses on globalization and higher education, international and comparative higher education, and higher education and social inequality. He is currently researching the implications of the worldwide trend to high participation systems of higher education.

Higher education as self-formation[1]

Introduction

Between 2004 and 2009, the author and colleagues engaged in data collection among international students in Australia and New Zealand. Almost three hundred students were interviewed; four-fifths were from East Asia, Southeast Asia, and South Asia, and all were enrolled in degree-length programmes. Extended semi-structured interviews are a conversation in which the object of the research, the interviewee, has some scope to introduce new concepts and unexpected topics, and becomes one of the subjects of research. This methodological framing helped us to think differently about the students and their education.

The perspective that dominates the psychological research on cross-border education, especially where there is cultural difference, is that of 'adjustment'. In this paradigm, international education is understood as a journey from home country culture to host country culture, facilitated by growing language proficiency and cross-cultural encounters. International students progress by acquiring the local attributes necessary to psychological well-being and academic success. The host country culture is normalized, the host country institutions are taken as given, and the international student is considered to be in deficit in the face of host country norms. The assimilationist adjustment paradigm is consistent with the long focus on population management in functionalist social science. Yet it often fails empirical tests and is contradicted by the students' sense of themselves. In research on international education, taken overall, there is no clear relation between academic success and the adoption of host country norms and values. Many students who maintain strong home identities, or are at ease with multiple identities, flourish in the country of education without adopting its ways (see, for example, Li and Gasser, 2005). Some of our student interviewees directly criticized the adjustment paradigm. They were often impressed by what they

---

1   This is the full text version. The spoken lecture was about one-third shorter.

saw in the country of education, were open to advice, and wanted to acquire local attributes necessary for success, without handing over their lives and their cultural identities for reprogramming.

All international students cross the border to become different, whether through learning, through the credential for which they study, by immersing themselves in a language, or simply by growing up. Often there is a person they want to become, though it is hard to truly see that person before this transformation happens. Most interviewees talked freely about the complex demands they faced living away from those they knew, amid problems of language and communication, academic work, university bureaucracy, immigration officials, the housing market, finances, and part-time work. Many also talked about different roles and identities they could take on, and how they had changed during their stay. Their situation should not be romanticized. Most were surviving amid conditions shaped by necessity rather than being happy educational tourists. Like all students, domestic or international, many faced financial challenges. Most of the non-white students had experienced discrimination or abuse. Yet it became clear that it was wrong to model these students as essentially other-formed, as 'adjusted' or not, as weak agents in deficit, being moulded by stronger structures and wiser agency in the country of education. As Catherine Montgomery (2010) also found, in the ethnographic study of international students in UK that she conducted at much the same time as our research in Australia/New Zealand, international students were strong agents piloting the course of their own lives, albeit under circumstances they did not control. These students were engaged not in other-formation but in *self-formation*. And some of them spoke brilliantly, reflexively, about the joys and terrors of self-formation as a practice of self-determining human freedom (Marginson, 2014).

These findings suggested to me to two further lines of investigation. First, it is apparent that in a world in which, given the size of the global middle classes, perhaps 25 to 30 per cent of people have the means to cross borders on a voluntary basis, there is a circular relation between mobility, self-formation, and freedom. There is research evidence on this. The OECD's (2016) *Perspectives on Global Development 2017: International migration in a shifting world* compares the cross-border mobility of people with and without university degrees. For those without degrees the tendency to move across borders is correlated to income. As income rises people are more likely to move. That is what common sense would expect. But among those with degrees the pattern is different. At a given income, those with degrees are more mobile than those without. In that respect higher education helps democratize mobility – though only providing you can get into higher education in the first place. In addition, among those with degrees, once a modest threshold income is reached, when income rises further there is little change in mobility. The propensity to travel is income inelastic. In helping graduates to achieve the confidence to move freely across the world, higher education weakens the effects of economic determinism on their imaginings, choices, and life trajectories. Degree-level education directly constitutes greater personal agential freedoms, without mediation by other factors. The balance between structure and agency is shifted, in favour of agency. This is a substantial gain.

Second, and most importantly, the implications are not confined to international students. Self-formation is especially visible among international students because they have little choice. They undergo substantial changes in compressed time periods, engage in rapid learning, make novel decisions, and constantly negotiate plural identities. However, the notion of students as reflexive and self-determining persons, expanding their own agency freedom, applies to all higher education and not just to international education.

Having reached it by an indirect route, via international education, it is this second line of argument that is pursued in this paper: the simple, far-reaching idea of *higher education as self-formation and the expansion of freedom*. By 'higher education' the paper refers to the educational process, not 'the university' or research. The practices of self-formation as freedom include all we might want from the higher educational process. I believe that this orientation to students and to learning-in-society is superior to the alternatives.

Higher education as self-formation rests on the irreducible fact that while learning is conditioned by external factors, by the learner's background and resources, the institution, the curriculum, teaching, and other circumstances, only the learner does the actual learning. It is also consistent with modernity itself, which for several intersecting reasons – including universal markets, political democracy, and mass education – has come to foreground identity and agency at this time in history over much of the world. Autonomous agency has been called the key concept of modernity (Kivelä, 2012: 65). In Anthony Giddens's words, modern life is a never-ending 'reflexive project of the self' (Giddens, 1991; Zhao and Biesta, 2011): consider career, consumption, conversation in social networks, fashion, body management, the preoccupation with cultural labels, the identity politics of left and right, even the selves matching selves in dating websites. In that respect self-formation is a more modernist idea than the notion of higher education that is suggested in mainstream psychology and economics, where the student is modelled as an empty vessel for others to fill, and where the value of that vessel, once filled, is taken to be shaped by the values generated in market exchange and not by the graduate's own objectives.

The remainder of the paper will attempt to ground this idea of higher education as self-formation in freedom. It works largely in educational philosophy, while drawing also on empirical examples to illustrate some points. First, the paper discusses notions of self-forming freedom in the works of Amartya Sen and Michel Foucault. Second, it reviews Confucian self-cultivation through learning, the Bildung tradition in Germany, and the American pragmatists, touching also on the immersion in knowledge fundamental to self-formation in higher education. Third, it considers the most difficult piece of the puzzle: the relations between individual self-formation and social formation, which is here called socially nested self-formation. Finally, the paper compares higher education as self-formation to other constructions of the student trajectory, such as investment in human capital, or social position, and the idea of the student as consumer. Higher education as self-formation does what the consumption paradigm pretends to do, but does not do. It puts the student at the centre of the frame.

Agency freedom

No idea is more potent for us than freedom. In institutions that are devoted to education we care also about equality and solidarity, yet this is mostly because we want everyone to have access to positive and negative freedoms, broadly defined, and their conditions and means. Freedom is the heart of the political cultures shaped by the French Revolution, including Anglo-American political cultures. This in turn drives the never wholly resolved tension between the individual and the social that is inherent in those political cultures.

Though there are many accounts of freedom, Amartya Sen's account of self-determination is especially helpful. If identity is what a person understands themselves or others to be, an 'agent', states Sen, is 'someone who acts and brings about change, and whose achievements can be judged in terms of her own values and objectives, whether or not we assess them in terms of some external criteria as well' (Sen, 2000: 19). Sen remarks that 'responsible adults must be in charge of their own well-being; it is for them to decide how to use their capabilities'. The initial step in understanding self-formation in higher education is to assume students are self-responsible adults rather than dependent children.

Beyond that, Sen's notion of human freedom has three elements. First is the freedom of the individual from external threat, coercion, or constraint. Sen calls this 'control freedom'; it roughly corresponds to the notion of negative freedom in the work of Isaiah Berlin (1969). Second comes freedom as the capacity of the individual to act, which depends on capabilities and resources, and on social arrangements that enable people to put their choices into practice. Sen calls this 'freedom as power', and in later work 'effective freedom' (Sen, 1985, 1992). Others call it positive freedom. Third is 'agency freedom', the active human will, the seat of self-directed conscious action, which guides reflexive self-formation and the self-negotiation of identity. Agency is about being 'master of my fate' and 'captain of my soul', as in *Invictus* by William Ernest Henley, the poem that sustained Nelson Mandela's sense of himself during his 27 years in a South African prison.[2] Agency freedom moves beyond a utilitarian calculus of net economic advantage to take in virtue, including status, dignity, family, friends, making things, satisfying work, the scope to realize forms of life, and shared collective goods as well as individual goods. Sen's three elements of freedom are interdependent. Control freedom and effective freedom can be understood as defensive and proactive moments of agency.

Sen also states that a person's capabilities 'depend on the nature of the social arrangements, which can be crucial for individual freedoms' (Sen, 2000: 288). Inequality, poverty, and discrimination stratify the agency of individuals and groups. Yet in the agency perspective structural determination is not absolute. Structures are always partly open, closed systems sit within larger open systems, and structural determination is disrupted by contingency and by agency. Agency is not just a modernist trope; it is the way through for disadvantaged populations, as Sue Clegg (2011) points out. Michel Foucault remarks that the self is the only object that one can freely will 'without having to take into consideration external determinations' (Foucault, 2005: 133). He locates agency 'in the constant interplay between strategies of power and resistance' (Foucault, cited in Ball, 2017: 55). Margaret Archer notes that while structure and agency are interdependent they are not identical; the relationship can vary (Jessop, 2005: 47). Human reflexivity mediates between structure and agency (see discussion in Dyke, 2015: 549). Here, because higher

---

2   The last of the four stanzas of *Invictus* reads: 'It matters not how strait the gate, | How charged with punishments the scroll, | I am the master of my fate, | I am the captain of my soul.'

education enhances the capacity for reflexivity, and thereby expands the scope for agency, it grows the space for freedom.

In fact, higher education advances all three of Sen's aspects of freedom, especially effective freedom, the capacity of the individual to act, and agency freedom. We have seen this in relation to mobility. The OECD (2015) publishes further data on the contribution of higher education to graduate agency. There is a close association between graduation and possessing skills in information and communications technology: electronic sociability. People who complete tertiary education are much more likely to believe they have a say in government than are people who left formal education before upper secondary school. Graduates more often report that they trust people, manage money with greater confidence, and so on.

Let's turn from Sen to another way into higher education, self-formation, and freedom: the last three of Foucault's annual lectures to the College de France (1981 to 1984). For Foucault, as Stephen Ball puts it, 'freedom is the capacity and opportunity to participate in one's self-formation' (Ball, 2017: 69). Foucault knows about the openness of the present, and tells people they are 'much freer than they feel' (Ball, 2017: 35), but he is also at pains to emphasize that freedom is a process of struggle (Ball, 2017: 69) and an often arduous 'work of the self on the self, an elaboration of the self by the self, a progressive transformation of the self by the self' (Foucault, 2005: 93).

In the late lectures, in what might be called the post-governmentality years, Foucault shifted his project from the history of the docile subject of domination, whose individuality is regulated by the normalizing practices of the state, to the history of the active subject and the potential for a freedom in which one can become something that one was not (Ball, 2017: xv, 55, 61). Foucault is most concerned about control freedom in Sen's sense, freedom from determination by the state. The development of an 'ethic of the self' is an 'indispensable task', he states. 'There is no first or final point of resistance to political power other than in the relationship one has to oneself' (Foucault, 2005: 251). To rethink the autonomous subject, Foucault renews his thought by using the same methodological device as was employed to such marked effect in both the Renaissance and the Enlightenment: he returns to the Classical world. He reviews the 'great culture of self' that evolved in the Hellenistic and Roman worlds between Plato's fourth century BCE in Athens and the fourth century CE in Rome (Foucault, 2005: 50). In these centuries the care of oneself became seen as 'a permanent obligation for every individual' throughout life and as its own end, without the constraints of mediating institutions or objectives (Foucault, 2005: 37, 83). This contrasted with the Christian period that followed, with its theme of the renunciation of the self. Within Christian belief individuals had to subordinate themselves to God and his ministers, in order to find the way to know and to care for themselves (Foucault, 2005: 70–1). In the shift back to a self that was mediated by the external agent, people were rendered less free than their classical predecessors. However, Hellenic and Roman autonomy was achieved only by hard work of the self on the self. Foucault discusses various practices of the autonomous self, including meditation, rituals of self-examination, rules of ethical conduct, truth-telling (*parrhesia*), and forms of the 'other life' as practised by the Stoics and Cynics. He notes that while 'the theme of return to the self' recurs in modern culture, as yet 'I do not think we have anything to be proud of in our current efforts to reconstitute an ethic of the self' (Foucault, 2005: 251).

Foucault's 'return to the self' was his final reckoning – for in the late lectures he knew that he was dying – with the ambiguous legacy of the Enlightenment. Foucault maintained his lifelong refusal to subscribe to Immanuel Kant's transcendental rules of truth. At the same time, he attached himself to the other, more transformative side of the Kantian inheritance, 'the "critical" legacy' embodied in Kant's essay 'What is Enlightenment?', where philosophy, working on itself, challenges the present on the basis of its insights into the times, into what we are (Foucault, 2010; Gross, cited in Foucault, 2010: 379). The recurring cycle of criticism and transformation enlarges both the self-space and the social space of freedom. But to understand the Enlightenment tradition of criticism and self-criticism it was essential to understand its older Greek and Roman roots, the original forms of reflexive criticism. Foucault identifies two primary methods of criticism. The Platonists held out the 'other world' as the point of reference against which this world could be critically judged. For the Cynics, if life was truly a life of truth, 'must it not be an *other* life, a life which is radically and paradoxically other?' (Foucault, 2011: 245). In self-formation we place ourselves in doubt, and in this lies new possibilities (Ball, 2017: 56). This leads Foucault to his terminal insight, the last sentence in the last lecture on 28 March 1984:

> But what I would like to stress in conclusion is this: there is no establishment of the truth without an essential position of otherness; the truth is never the same; there can be truth only in the form of the other world and the other life ('l'autre monde et de la vie autre').

> (Foucault, 2011: 340)

What is the relevance of all this to higher education? First, relevance lies in the focus on self-formation. Ball notes that while education is 'one of the key sites in which the processes of normalisation are enacted', it can also become 'a locus of struggle for productive processes of self-formation and freedom' (Ball, 2017: 3). Second, this material presents us with Foucault's final challenging idea, taking us to the outer reaches of creative agency: in self-formation we can become something other than we are, and find a truth that is necessarily other, different. At best, higher education incubates student projects of otherness. Third, Foucault's idea here of self-transformation resonates with the Bildung idea in education (as he notes; Foucault, 2005: 610), while his specific focus on self-transformation through the painstaking work of self on self resonates also with Confucian self-cultivation (which he does not mention). As in Greece and Rome, self-formation in higher education has been modelled in the form of specific practices, some of them as old as Greece and Rome. It is time to look at these.

Self-cultivation

The idea of self-formation in education has been taken up in varying ways in different cultures (Zhao and Biesta, 2011: 3). The oldest practice is Confucian self-cultivation. Zhao and Deng state that 'the idea of person-making is at the heart of the Confucian heritage of educational thinking. It has long been held that self-cultivation is the precondition' for developing 'the critical and creative potential of the individual and enabling him or her to fulfil social responsibilities and functions' (Zhao and Deng, 2016: 2–3). In a comparison of self-formation East and West, Zhao and Biesta remark that the Confucian self is not a finished entity but engaged in a continuous process of self-perfection (Zhao and Biesta, 2011: 13). Education cannot be separated from 'becoming an ideal and genuine human person' (Zhao and Deng, 2016: 3). 'Confucianism presents a view of identity and the self that is much more explicitly informed by moral and ethical dimensions' (Zhao and Biesta, 2011: 9). Classic Confucian education embodies a strong commitment to the common good. It also serves the state, and emphasizes effective freedom and agency freedom more than it emphasizes freedom as control, the freedom independent of (and, if necessary, against) the state that is the main focus in the Anglo-American countries.

Dong Zhongshu, who established Confucianism as the theoretical foundation of the Han state, proposed the first imperial academy, Taixue, in

124 BCE (Yang, 2017). Traditional higher education in China did not take the form of incorporated universities, as in Europe, which worked in a variable semi-independent space between church and state. Instead China channelled self-cultivation into training and selection for the state bureaucracy. Yet the Confucian idea of *Ren*, humanity in the broad sense, is at the heart of Chinese self-formation. Weiming Tu states that 'the great strength of modern East Asia is its … self-definition as a learning civilization', which may be 'the most precious legacy of Confucian humanism' (Tu, 2013: 334). Ren is therefore one element feeding into China's distinctively 'compressed' (Ulrich Beck, 2016: 265) form of modernization (Tu, 1996: 59–61). Yet with state-driven instrumentalism and Western neoliberalism also in play, others are less optimistic than Tu. Zhao and Deng question whether higher education in China has retained the classical commitment to holistic person-forming, or has collapsed into economic utility and a focus on credentials rather than learning content (Zhao and Deng, 2016: 2–3).

This coincides with the critique of instrumentalism in the West. At the same time, the East–West similarities in education should not be overstated. Certainly, there are important differences in self-formation. Jin Li uses learner word association to compare beliefs about learning among students in China and the United States. In Li's 2003 study using this method, American students were more reflexive about learners' mental functioning, and inquiry and imagination, and referred more to external conditions that affected learning (mostly to limit it). The Chinese focused less on external conditions, and emphasized how learners actively seek learning on their own, underlining intrinsic motivation and learner agency (Li, 2003: 263; see also Hayhoe, 2017: 7). They were also more normative, talking about learning in terms of attitudes and action, and hardship, and virtues such as diligence and steadfastness – terms that never surfaced in American talk (Li, 2003: 261–2). The Chinese saw the practical purposes of higher education as important, yet learning and knowledge were also 'indispensable to their personal lives' and the path to becoming a better person (Li, 2003: 265). Like their forebears they cultivated themselves holistically in the moral domain, suggesting that there had been no thoroughgoing evacuation of traditional Confucian practices. Anne Shostya's study of business students in New York and Shanghai found that outside class Chinese students spent an average of 9.6 hours per week in reading and 22.3 hours in study, compared to American students' 4.4 hours of reading and 9.1 hours in study (Shostya, 2015: 201). In short, Chinese students are more focused than are their American counterparts on learning in Foucault's terms, through the lifelong work of 'self on self', albeit that this is a work partly mediated by educational institutions, curricula, and examinations.

Now to Bildung. One translation of the German word 'Bildung' is in fact 'self-formation'; other versions include 'development' and 'inner cultivation'. The concept though is larger than any of these and includes them all (Taylor, 2017: 3; Siljander and Sutinen, 2012: 2). Though the Bildung idea emerged in eighteenth-century Western Europe at a time when reformed European school systems were touched by the curriculum and examination system in distant China, Bildung had indigenous roots in the post-feudal Enlightenment thought of Immanuel Kant, Jean-Jacques Rousseau, and others. 'Self-formation' in Kant's definition of the Enlightenment meant 'man's release from his self-incurred tutelage through the exercise of his own understanding' (Biesta, 2002: 345). The role of education was to cultivate the inner self in both intellectual and ethical terms, so as to form citizens in public rationality who would constitute the emerging civil society (Biesta, 2002: 345; Foucault, 2010: 26). Kant emphasized that Bildung would not occur by itself; it required education. Education was 'the crucial element for evolving humanity, which takes its place in every individual, but also on the collective level' (Kivelä, 2012: 59–60). Reason would not emerge spontaneously. The process rested on training and teaching (Kivelä, 2012). Once they reached the stage of full autonomy, the educated individuals together would drive the collective modernization of society, in which the common understanding would advance in correspondence with the continuous improvement of institutions.

Bildung resembled Confucian self-cultivation in being a holistic project with a strong moral dimension that was joined to systematic learning practices, though Bildung placed greater emphasis on the autonomous will, on agency freedom (Taylor, 2017: 5), and on freedom as control: importantly, it also focused on civil society rather than the state. Kant emphasized the need for people to learn to think independently without guidance from the authorities (Kivelä, 2012: 62). Bildung promised liberation from power structures, while the universal curriculum also offered a potential escape from the limiting effects of social background. Nevertheless, like Confucianism in the Han dynasty, Bildung was co-opted for nation-building. An example of this can be found in Wilhelm von Humboldt's formula for the University of Berlin. Von Humboldt wanted to institute a formative curriculum that was broad and deep, grounded in history, classical languages and literature, linguistics, science, and research (Kirby and van der Wende, 2016: 2–3), while at the same time placing the university in the service of the state. He sought to preserve the original idea of education that was free of social, economic, and political constraints by prescribing full university autonomy and the freedom to learn and to teach: *Lernfreiheit* and *Lehrfreiheit*. Across the world academics continue to defend their self-determination by invoking the global culture of the Humboldtian university (Siljander and Sutinen, 2012: 15); though this has become primarily focused on the control freedom of the academic, rather than the self-formation of the autonomous student.

Bildung implies an educational process dedicated to being and becoming, to the open-ended evolution of human potential, not static measures of skills and knowledge. Its notion of perfectibility resembles Confucian self-cultivation in that the goal is never achieved. Rather, self-formation opens new horizons as it proceeds, and the educability of the self-forming learner is not fixed but is continually expanding (Siljander, 2012: 94). Teaching and learning cannot be exhaustively defined in terms of cause and effect, for there is always 'an open independent space', independent of the teacher, for self-formation by the student (Siljander, 2012: 96). This space is not wholly sufficient in itself. Teaching, educational structures, and the larger socio-cultural world continue to matter. The core notion of Bildung, of educational subjects shaped by context but with powers of self-determination, developing themselves through their own actions so as to achieve a more advanced form of life (Siljander and Sutinen, 2012: 3–4), retains its vitality – though contemporary advocates of Bildung tend to set aside the Enlightenment claim to a singular rationality, and mostly prefer to join the Kantian project to other educational practices that recognize difference and diversity (Taylor, 2017: 3; Biesta, 2002).

The American pragmatists, who were influenced by German education and the Bildung tradition, agreed that the purpose of education was the formation of the free autonomous self. In their summary of Bildung, Siljander and Sutinen find that 'Dewey's *Democracy and Education* is, basically, a theory of Bildung', especially where he writes about 'self-discipline' and a curriculum of 'humanistic and naturalistic studies' (Siljander and Sutinen, 2012: 16). The pragmatists also gave self-formation their own twist. Their central principle was 'growth' (Kivelä *et al.*, 2012: 207). Self-realizing mental formation occurred through inquiry, activity, and experience; in natural and cultural environments; through shared language, learned reflexivity, and growing harmony with the environmental setting (Väkevä, 2012). More recent interpretations of pragmatism have partly shifted the balance from the intentional activity of the teacher to the development of self-regulation by the self-forming learner (Kivelä *et al.*, 2012: 308).

There are two factors that distinguish self-formation in higher education from the many other sites in which self-formation takes place: the role of the academic teacher, and the immersion in knowledges. In relation to teaching, Kant noted the paradox inherent in teaching learners to form themselves: 'How is it possible to cultivate freedom by coercion?' (Pikkarainen, 2012: 21).[3] The dilemma is less pressing in higher education than at school level, as in higher education the teacher is the facilitator of already autonomous learners. Immersion in knowledge is the more important signifier of higher education, even though educational policy often pays little attention to the formative effects of knowledge (Ashwin, 2014: 123).

Referencing Basil Bernstein (2000), Paul Ashwin focuses on transitions between 'knowledge-as research, knowledge-as-curriculum and knowledge-as-student-understanding' (Ashwin, 2014: 124). These transitions are often contested and are contextually variant. Tracking these transitions empirically 'offers a powerful way of gaining a sense of the transformative power of higher education because it brings into focus the ways in which higher education transforms students' understanding and identities' (Ashwin, 2014: 124); or rather, it brings into focus the ways that students transform themselves through the immersion in knowledge. Working within particular bodies of knowledge, students acquire the different 'gazes' and 'lenses' required to access each knowledge (Ashwin, 2014: 125), and may also acquire the distinctive values associated with the particular academic or professional discipline. Each body of knowledge leaves distinctive traces in the self-formation process.

In a study of sociology students' accounts of their discipline and the way those accounts change over the course of the degree, Paul Ashwin, Andrea Abbas, and Monica McLean demonstrate that over time most students move to a more relational understanding of the discipline and of society (Ashwin et al., 2014: 224–5). The authors cite Dubet's comment that students 'form themselves through the meaning they attribute to knowledge' (Ashwin et al., 2014: 222). The researchers also find that engaging with knowledge alone is

---

3   Kant wrote: 'One of the greatest problems of education is how to unite submission to the necessary restraint with the child's capability of exercising his free will – for restraint is necessary. How am I to develop the sense of freedom in spite of the restraint? I am to accustom my person to endure a restraint on his freedom, and at the same time I am to guide him to use his freedom aright. Without this all education is merely mechanical, and the child, when his education is over, will never be able to make a possible use of his freedom' (see Kivelä, 2012: 66). Kant saw it as essential to acknowledge the freedom of the child from the beginning, while also showing the child that the exercise of his or her own freedom depended on the child supporting the freedom of others (Kivelä, 2012: 68).

not sufficient to secure a transformation of the student's perspective: 'There also needs to be an alignment between students' personal projects and the focus of disciplinary knowledge' (Ashwin *et al.*, 2014: 231), which highlights the role of agency freedom in knowledge-based learning. Separately, Ashwin and McVitty note that while 'knowledge transforms students as they engage with it … students also transform knowledge as they make sense of it' (Ashwin and McVitty, 2015). The mutually transformative effects of self-forming subjects and knowledge are a rich domain for further research inquiry.

Social formation

The student self is continuously created in a shifting combination of (1) the given material conditions, (2) the social relations in which the student is embedded and which he or she is a partner in making, and (3) the agency freedom or active will of the student. All student self-formation is historically grounded and subject to relations of power, and like all localized practices it is specific to contexts. What, then, can be said in general terms? The above account suggests that the idea of higher education as self-formation, in at least some sense, is widely understood. The more difficult issue is the character of socially nested self-formation – that is, the relation between self-formation in higher education and the larger social setting, and especially the formative social effects of higher education (its role in social formation). This is often seen as a normative question: what kind of social relations or values should be the horizon of the educational project of self-formation (Zhao and Biesta, 2011: 6–8)? Yet it is also an empirical question: what kind of social relations optimize self-formation, and vice versa?

In Lev Vygotsky's studies in social psychology (see, for example, Vygotsky, 1978) the individual child develops the self and social relations as part of the same process. Strikingly, the infant often exercises sufficient agency to draw adults into speech exchange. Early speech in turn builds the child's social identity and enhances capability, further augmenting agency. The medium for this process, the point of mediation between individual and social, is language, which establishes socially recognized identity and is both a shared and an individualizable property. Out of the experience of speech community the mentality of the child is patterned and she/he learns to work with and on her/his own mind, enabling reflexivity. 'The true development of thinking is not from the individual to the social, it is from the social to the individual,' states

Vygotsky (1986: 36). '*An interpersonal process is transformed into an intrapersonal one*. Every function in the child's cultural development appears twice, first, on the social level, and later, on the individual level' (Vygotsky, 1978: 57; emphasis in original). The social, historically prior to the individual, provides the material essential for individual self-formation.

Likewise for C.P. Mead, an American near-contemporary of Vygotsky, individual growth or self-formation takes place through mutual exchange in social settings through the medium of language. Individuals create shared meanings or solve problems, triggering reflection (Siljander and Sutinen, 2012: 6, 11, 16; Biesta, 2012: 248). Margaret Kettle illustrates the crucial role of language in mediating self-formation. Her interview subject, a Thai student studying in Australia, believed that his effective agency did not exist until he learned to communicate and interact effectively with local persons (Kettle, 2005).

Both Bildung and Confucian self-cultivation emphasize the interdependency of the individual and social, with each doing so in a distinctive way. According to Ari Kivelä, in the Kantian version of Bildung the aim of education is 'the active autonomous person within the framework of social life', a rational subject who uses reason in a public way and 'lives in the public sphere among other individual beings' (Kivelä, 2012: 59; see also Kontio, 2012: 33). For Fichte, as for Vygotsky, Mead, and Dewey later, 'self-consciousness and interpersonal relations emerge only simultaneously' (Kivelä, 2012: 78). However, while the social is built onto the individual in Bildung, perhaps the scaffolding could be dismantled. Civil society appears as both more abstract and more normative than is the local domain of learning. Von Humboldt is one whose take on Bildung appears lopsided, overly individualistic (Konrad, 2012: 120). Some contemporary advocates of Bildung propose that education should place greater emphasis on interdependent social relations (for example, Taylor, 2017: 13–14; Zhao and Biesta, 2011: 6).

At times the American pragmatists are clearer about the reciprocity between the individual and social. For Dewey, the terms 'social' and 'individual' are 'hopelessly ambiguous' – but only when they are placed in antithesis (Dewey, 1927: 186). Still, the individual/social tension in self-formation is not quite as easily dismissed, nor easily resolved. On one hand, it is significant that in the general culture, and to a lesser extent in education, self-formation is mostly practised without sufficient regard either to the social determinants of individual potential, or to the common good. It is essential to acknowledge the socially contextualized character of individual formation, the way that individuals, and groups, are nested in a much larger lattice of social exchange, in which the resources and capabilities of self-formation are unevenly distributed. On the other hand, learning is individually appropriated, and the imagining individual has the potential to lift above her or his context. In short, individual agency is always both socially separated *and* socially embedded. This double coding of the self is one of the distinctive achievements of Anglo-American–European thought. It widens the scope to respond to Foucault's final challenge – the scope for a creative agency that first translates itself into otherness, into seeing and doing differently, and then brings that otherness back to challenge, disturb, and otherwise enrich the social realm.

On the whole, the social dimension is more consistently central to Confucian thought than it is to Bildung. Confucian ideas about education have always been relational in form and content, and the framing is more consistently normative than it is in Bildung. *Ren* exists in relationships. In Chinese, the word 'Ren' combines the word for 'two' and the word for 'human being'. According to Zhao and Biesta, 'Confucius cared about a person's individual development, but strongly maintained that it should take place in the context of human relationships' (Zhao and Biesta, 2011: 11). They also cite Sun, for whom the Confucian view of self has three aspects: the 'I' undivided with the universe, the 'I' in unity with other human beings, and the wholeness of 'I' with self that enables the reflexive work of self on self (Zhao and Biesta, 2011; Sun, 2008). Confucian self-cultivation in education means the cultivation of all three types of relationship.

Hence in Confucian education we find on one hand the direct, unmediated reflexivity, the work of self on self, as in the Stoics of the Hellenic period described by Foucault. On the other hand there are also forms of reflexivity that are mediated, in two different ways: first, through personal relationships; second, through engagement in the world as a whole – *Tianxia*, all under heaven, the global public good in its largest sense. The self-formation project can be continually monitored using all three forms of reflexivity. Adapting the classic Confucian text *The Great Learning*, the neo-Confucianism of the Song Dynasty identified eight stages to the realization of self-cultivation: 'Investigating things; extending one's knowledge; making one's intentions sincere; rectifying one's mind; cultivating one's personal life; regulating one's family; governing one's state; and setting the world at peace and harmony' (Chai, 2016: 75).

At the same time, in a normative approach to the social there are potential dilemmas for educational self-formation. It is one matter for education to move beyond methodological individualism to foreground the relational, the contextual, and the ecological, as it should do. It is another matter for education to fill the content of the social with its preferred version of social relations and maximize its normative power. Driving a single social philosophy through higher education would violate all three of Sen's freedoms.

Other explanations

The idea of higher education as self-formation is challenged by alternative explanations of higher education, some of which have greater traction in policy. In a paper published in 2015, Ashwin, Abbas and McLean examine the ways in which 'high-quality' higher education is represented in the policy-related documents of government and other actors in the UK. They find that there are two broad types of representations. First is the 'dominant market-oriented generic discourse', in which quality is secured through the consumer power of students in a competitive market of producer institutions. That is very familiar. Second, they identify a more fragmented set of discourses that acknowledge transformation in higher education. In this second group, disciplinary knowledge and critical thinking are mentioned but the main emphasis is on teaching (Ashwin *et al.*, 2015: 610); that is, on higher education primarily as other-formation rather than self-formation. It is striking that overall, in the dominant discourse and the alternate discourses taken together, both knowledge and student formation are downplayed, and agency-driven self-formation is absent – despite the rhetoric of student-centredness that is part of the consumption paradigm. The researchers comment that even the alternate discourses do not 'give a sense of what is special about the knowledge that students are engaging with' or 'give a sense of the identities that they develop through this engagement' (Ashwin *et al.*, 2015: 619).

This pattern of discourse says more about the ideological nature of policy discussion than about the potentials of higher education. When compared to Bildung, John Dewey, and Confucian self-cultivation, the generic market-consumer paradigm drastically shrinks what higher education offers, its value to individuals and societies. In the UK the consumer paradigm narrows the practical agenda to immediate student satisfaction, short-term graduate salaries, and doubtful probabilistic judgements about long-term individual outcomes for graduates. The consumer paradigm is not psychologically sophisticated. It assumes that students salivate at market signals, like Pavlov's *sobaka* with just one thing on its mind – food. As Ashwin and McVitty remark, the consumer paradigm asks students to commodify their own processes of intellectual and personal transformation. It does so without guaranteeing them material rewards, for they remain hostage to fortune; there is little real agency on offer (Ashwin and McVitty, 2015), for how much power do mass consumers ever exercise? Fortunately, we know students have a less consumptionist take on higher education than policy has. In the UK a survey of 9,000 students at 123 institutions, funded by a consortium of student unions, found 34 per cent of respondents believed universities should be accountable for poor graduate employment figures but 68 per cent believed they were accountable for poor teaching. When asked which factors demonstrate that a university has excellent teaching, graduate employment was ranked last out of seven options (Trendence UK, 2017). In other words, most students have not bought into the idea of the nexus between teaching quality, satisfaction, employment, and choice of university. They don't self-form while shopping at Tesco, or not much. They do self-form in higher education.

And yet: the market paradigm is not to be dismissed entirely. The idea of higher education as an investment in future graduate productivity or in human capital, and the idea that completing a degree enhances employability, are by no means always wrong. In some courses, especially in the bounded professions, it is possible to make realistic estimates of lifetime earnings. Some students, some of the time, make decisions about higher education according to human capital theory's economic calculus. No doubt nearly all students hope that their degree will at least enhance their economic prospects. Some see themselves as consumers, and behave accordingly;[4] in a policy setting that defines higher education as consumption such behaviours will become more prevalent over time (see, for students in the UK, Tomlinson, 2017). Likewise, the idea of society as a field of investment in positional goods has salience. Many if not most families see in higher education the potential to maintain or uplift their social position. And no doubt some students want to secure Bourdieuian social and cultural capitals as forms of private benefit.

There are also many other ways in which students expand themselves, their resources, and their projects. Some love the subjects they study and find knowledge to be an end in itself. Some are looking for suitable marriage partners. Some are intensively engaged in cultural or political action on campus. Some

---

4   Studies of student motivation often find that the consumption perspective is present but not dominant. For example, in relation to study abroad, Jæger and Gram (2017).

have a passion for the common good and imagine themselves working on global problems in future. Many are simply 'finding themselves' while moving into adult life. Some want to please their families, self-forming themselves in other-determined ways. And, typically, students nurture more than one of these different higher education projects at the same time—and they position their higher education projects in different ways, as immediate gratification, as investment, and as identity. For example, many students studying mentally expanding disciplines like philosophy have shelved the thorny question of where it is taking them, or not, but most philosophy students also want a good job after graduation.

'Some', 'many', 'much', 'most'. Not 'all'. None of these paradigms applies to all students, all of the time, everywhere. None is a universal or sufficient explanation of higher education. Yet that is how human capital theory, the consumer paradigm, the theory of positional goods, Bourdieu's capitals, even liberal education, present themselves to us: as contending claims for the status of single transcendent truth. Each claim is holistic in its would-be reach. Yet it is grounded in a partial slice of the world. The framing of higher education should encompass all of these phenomena, each of these different constellations of ideas and practices, without elevating any one to dominance. The common element – the centre of the inquiry into the higher education process – is the self-forming student. The inclusive framework is higher education as self-formation, and self-formation as the expansion of freedom. Self-formation includes all the different ways that students build agency and extend their effective freedoms by augmenting themselves. When higher education as self-formation is extended into higher education as socially nested self-formation, the inquiry can take in the augmentation of others, and the common good.

Conclusions

This paper has argued that higher education is comprised of processes of student self-formation, and that student self-formation is a practice of freedom. In different forms, student self-formation has a long history in education; though the idea as such has little current policy support, it is widely understood, especially in East Asia where education often goes deeper than elsewhere in the world. Self-formation is our best explanation and practice of higher education. The way forward is to build on it.

Like all large ideas in education, such as equality of opportunity, self-formation is both a norm that is pursued and a living empirical reality. It is open-ended, it is about potential more than outcomes, and its practices are always incomplete. However, self-formation is both necessary and sufficient to understand higher education. It takes in all the ways that students augment themselves. As socially nested self-formation, it can take in all the ways in which the self-formation of students contributes to ongoing social formation. However, while it is possible to secure a universal agreement on the notion of self-formation (as was the case, for example, in traditional China), consensus on the social is more elusive.

Self-formation is piloted by student agency, and this varies. Agency is socially situated, located in particular places, exhibits differentiated resources, and tends to change over time (Ashwin and McVitty, 2015: 3). As Sen (1985) points out, economic well-being is an insufficient foundation for freedom. The agency perspective takes in a larger set of goals and virtues in higher education.

Once self-formation is positioned as the heart of higher education, student-centred learning can be more fully developed (there are no guarantees; some self-cultivation coexists with authoritarian pedagogies). This positioning also changes the customary methods for understanding higher education. First, students become understood as the primary unit of analysis. Second, disciplines, sets of knowledge, may become as important as institutions because of the role of knowledge in shaping agency.

Which practices, then, can build student freedoms? Fostering the agency freedom of students and its scope to act is *the* key to self-formation. In addition, expanding the space in which students are free of constraint and coercion, for example by reducing authoritarian administration or promoting less discriminatory practices, enhances freedom as control. Resources and opportunities, such as information, affordable housing, and mobility, augment effective freedom. Note also that higher education is only one of the social domains in which students form themselves. The effectiveness of higher education is optimized when self-formation in higher education is in synchrony with self-formation in these other domains, for example the home, work, and social communications.

In research, there is scope for empirical investigation into the mix and match of each student's particular projects of self-formation, and into variations in self-formation, its resources, and its strategies, by country, class, culture, gender, and over time. There is also scope to explore how immersion in knowledge, evolving competences, growing self-efficacy, and changing values feeds agency freedom and develops the portfolio of potential personal projects (Klemencic, 2015). And there is inquiry into those techniques in higher education that already, now, open the way to forms of truth of the other world and the other life, as Foucault puts it: truths that enable us to become radically other. How is it that by working on ourselves in higher education, pushing through our limits, we can make a new self and a new world?

References

Ashwin, P. (2014) 'Knowledge, curriculum and student understanding in higher education'. *Higher Education*, 67 (2), 123–6.

Ashwin, P., Abbas, A. and McLean, M. (2014) 'How do students' accounts of sociology change over the course of their undergraduate degrees?'. *Higher Education*, 67 (2), 219–34.

Ashwin, P., Abbas, A. and McLean, M. (2015) 'Representations of a high-quality system of undergraduate education in English higher education policy documents'. *Studies in Higher Education*, 40 (4), 610–23.

Ashwin, P. and McVitty, D. (2015) 'The meanings of student engagement: Implications for policies and practices'. In Curaj, A., Matei, L., Pricopie, R., Salmi, J. and Scott, P. (eds) *The European Higher Education Area: Between critical reflections and future policies*. Cham: Springer, 343–59.

Ball, S.J. (2017) *Foucault as Educator*. Cham: Springer.

Beck, U. (2016) 'Varieties of second modernity and the cosmopolitan vision'. *Theory, Culture and Society*, 33 (7–8), 257–70.

Berlin, I. (1969) 'Two concepts of liberty'. In Berlin, I. *Four Essays on Liberty*. London: Oxford University Press, 118–72.

Bernstein, B. (2000) *Pedagogy, Symbolic Control and Identity: Theory, research, critique*. Rev. ed. Lanham, MD: Rowman and Littlefield.

Biesta, G. (2002) 'Bildung and modernity: The future of Bildung in a world of difference'. *Studies in Philosophy and Education*, 21 (4–5), 343–51.

Biesta, G. (2012) 'George Herbert Mead: Formation through communication'. In Siljander, P., Kivelä, A. and Sutinen, A. (eds) *Theories of Bildung and Growth: Connections and controversies between continental educational thinking and American pragmatism*. Rotterdam: Sense Publishers, 247–60.

Chai, W.Y. (2016) 'Adapting the Western model of liberal arts education in China: The cases of Fudan University and Lingnan University'. In Jung, I., Nishimura, M. and Sasao, T. (eds) *Liberal Arts Education and Colleges in East Asia: Possibilities and challenges in the global age*. Singapore: Springer, 75–86.

Clegg, S. (2011) 'Cultural capital and agency: Connecting critique and curriculum in higher education'. *British Journal of Sociology of Education*, 32 (1), 93–108.

Dewey, J. (1927) *The Public and Its Problems*. Denver: Swallow Press.

Dubet, F. (2000) 'The sociology of pupils'. *Journal of Education Policy*, 15 (1), 93–104.

Dyke, M. (2015) 'Reconceptualising learning as a form of relational reflexivity'. *British Journal of Sociology of Education*, 36 (4), 542–57.

Foucault, M. (2005) *The Hermeneutics of the Subject: Lectures at the Collège de France, 1981–1982*. Ed. Gros, F. Trans. Burchell, G. New York: Palgrave Macmillan.

Foucault, M. (2010) *The Government of Self and Others: Lectures at the Collège de France, 1982–1983*. Ed. Gros, F. Trans. Burchell, G. Basingstoke: Palgrave Macmillan.

Foucault, M. (2011) *The Courage of the Truth (The Government of Self and Others II): Lectures at the Collège de France, 1983–1984*. Ed. Gros, F. Trans. Burchell, G. Basingstoke: Palgrave Macmillan.

Giddens, A. (1991) *Modernity and Self-Identity: Self and society in the late modern age*. Cambridge: Polity Press.

Hayhoe, R. (2017) 'China in the center: What will it mean for global education?'. *Frontiers of Education in China*, 12 (1), 3–28.

Jæger, K. and Gram, M. (2017) '"Totally different standards": Consumer orientation in study abroad contexts'. *Higher Education*, 74 (1), 33–47.

Jessop, B. (2005) 'Critical realism and the strategic-relational approach'. *New Formations*, 56, 40–53.

Kettle, M. (2005) 'Agency as discursive practice: From "nobody" to "somebody" as an international student in Australia'. *Asia Pacific Journal of Education*, 25 (1), 45–60.

Kirby, W.C. and van der Wende, M.C. (2016) 'A global dialogue on liberal arts and sciences: Re-engagement, re-imagination, and experimentation'. In Kirby, W.C. and van der Wende, M.C. (eds) *Experiences in Liberal Arts and Science Education from America, Europe, and Asia: A dialogue across continents*. New York: Palgrave Macmillan, 1–16.

Kivelä, A. (2012) 'From Immanuel Kant to Johann Gottlieb Fichte: Concept of education and German idealism'. In Siljander, P., Kivelä, A. and Sutinen, A. (eds) *Theories of Bildung and Growth: Connections and controversies between continental educational thinking and American pragmatism*. Rotterdam: Sense Publishers, 59–86.

Kivelä, A., Siljander, P. and Sutinen, A. (2012) 'Between Bildung and growth: Connections and controversies'. In Siljander, P., Kivelä, A. and Sutinen, A. (eds) *Theories of Bildung and Growth: Connections and controversies between continental educational thinking and American pragmatism*. Rotterdam: Sense Publishers, 303–12.

Klemencic, M. (2015) 'Introducing student agency into research on student engagement: An ontological explanation'. Unpublished paper. Cambridge, MA: Harvard University.

Konrad, F.-M. (2012) 'Wilhelm von Humboldt's contribution to a theory of Bildung'. In Siljander, P., Kivelä, A. and Sutinen, A. (eds) *Theories of Bildung and Growth: Connections and controversies between continental educational thinking and American pragmatism*. Rotterdam: Sense Publishers, 107–24.

Kontio, K. (2012) 'Jean-Jacques Rousseau on alienation, Bildung and education'. In Siljander, P., Kivelä, A. and Sutinen, A. (eds) *Theories of Bildung and Growth: Connections and controversies between continental educational thinking and American pragmatism*. Rotterdam: Sense Publishers, 31–46.

Li, A. and Gasser, M.B. (2005) 'Predicting Asian international students' sociocultural adjustment: A test of two mediation models'. *International Journal of Intercultural Relations*, 29 (5), 561–76.

Li, J. (2003) 'US and Chinese cultural beliefs about learning'. *Journal of Educational Psychology*, 95 (2), 258–67.

Marginson, S. (2014) 'Student self-formation in international education'. *Journal of Studies in International Education*, 18 (1), 6–22.

Montgomery, C. (2010) *Understanding the International Student Experience*. Basingstoke: Palgrave Macmillan.

OECD (Organization for Economic Co-operation and Development) (2015) *Education at a Glance 2015: OECD indicators*. Paris: OECD Publishing.

OECD (Organization for Economic Co-operation and Development) (2016) *Perspectives on Global Development 2017: International migration in a shifting world*. Paris: OECD Publishing. Online. www.oecd.org/dev/perspectives-on-global-development-22224475.htm (accessed 7 December 2017).

Pikkarainen, E. (2012) 'Signs of reality: The idea of general Bildung by J. A. Comenius'. In Siljander, P., Kivelä, A. and Sutinen, A. (eds) *Theories of Bildung and Growth: Connections and controversies between continental educational thinking and American pragmatism*. Rotterdam: Sense Publishers, 19–29.

Sen, A. (1985) 'Well-being, agency and freedom: The Dewey Lectures 1984'. *Journal of Philosophy*, 82 (4), 169–221.

Sen, A. (1992) *Inequality Reexamined*. Cambridge, MA: Harvard University Press.

Sen, A. (2000) *Development as Freedom*. New York: Anchor Books.

Shostya, A. (2015) 'The use of time among college students: A US–China comparison'. *International Journal of Education*, 7 (1), 195–208.

Siljander, P. (2012) 'Educability and Bildung in Herbart's theory of education'. In Siljander, P., Kivelä, A. and Sutinen, A. (eds) *Theories of Bildung and Growth: Connections and controversies between continental educational thinking and American pragmatism*. Rotterdam: Sense Publishers, 87–105.

Siljander, P. and Sutinen, A. (2012) 'Introduction'. In Siljander, P., Kivelä, A. and Sutinen, A. (eds) *Theories of Bildung and Growth: Connections and controversies between continental educational thinking and American pragmatism*. Rotterdam: Sense Publishers, 1–18.

Sun, Q. (2008) 'Confucian educational philosophy and its implication for lifelong learning and lifelong education'. *International Journal of Lifelong Education*, 27 (5), 559–78.

Taylor, C.A. (2017) 'Is a posthumanist Bildung possible? Reclaiming the promise of Bildung for contemporary higher education'. *Higher Education*, 74 (3), 419–35.

Tomlinson, M. (2017) 'Student perceptions of themselves as "consumers" of higher education'. *British Journal of Sociology of Education*, 38 (4), 450–67.

Trendence UK (2017) *Teaching Excellence: The student perspective*. London: Trendence UK. Online. http://wonkhe.com/wp-content/uploads/2017/11/tef-pr-research-report.pdf (accessed 7 December 2017).

Tu, W. (1996) 'Beyond the Enlightenment mentality: A Confucian perspective on ethics, migration, and global stewardship'. *International Migration Review*, 30 (1), 58–75.

Tu, W. (2013) 'Confucian humanism in perspective'. *Frontiers of Literary Studies in China*, 7 (3), 333–8.

Väkevä, L. (2012) 'Experiencing growth as a natural phenomenon: John Dewey's philosophy and the Bildung tradition'. In Siljander, P., Kivelä, A. and Sutinen, A. (eds) *Theories of Bildung and Growth: Connections and controversies between continental educational thinking and American pragmatism*. Rotterdam: Sense Publishers, 261–79.

Vygotsky, L.S. (1978) *Mind in Society: The development of higher psychological processes*. Ed. Cole, M. Cambridge, MA: Harvard University Press.

Vygotsky, L. (1986) *Thought and Language*. Translation rev. and ed. Kozulin, A. Cambridge, MA: MIT Press.

Yang, R. (2017) 'Transformations of higher education institutions in the Chinese tradition'. Unpublished paper. Hong Kong: University of Hong Kong.

Zhao, G. and Deng, Z. (2016) 'Introduction'. In Zhao, G. and Deng, Z. (eds) *Re-envisioning Chinese Education: The meaning of person-making in a new age*. London: Routledge, 1–9.

Zhao, K. and Biesta, G.J.J. (2011) 'Lifelong learning between "East" and "West": Confucianism and the reflexive project of the self'. *Interchange*, 42 (1), 1–20.